A DEFENSE OF POETRY

2001 AGNES LYNCH STARRETT PRIZE

Pitt Poetry Series
Ed Ochester, Editor

A DEFENSE OF POETRY

GABRIEL GUDDING

UNIVERSITY OF PITTSBURGH PRESS

The publication of this
book is supported by a
grant from the
Pennsylvania Council on
the Arts.

Published by the University of Pittsburgh Press,

Pittsburgh, Pa., 15260

Manufactured in the United States of America

Printed on acid-free paper

10 9 8 7 6 5 4 3 2 1

ISBN 0-8229-5786-8

for Mairéad Byrne

In hilaritas tristis, in tristitia hilaris.

GIORDANO BRUNO

This society might be characterized as a standing ovation
simultaneously in mourning.

CARLA HARRYMAN, *ANIMAL INSTINCTS*

The more helpless they are, the more instructive
are the examples they offer us.

PAUL KLEE

CONTENTS

A DEFENSE OF POETRY

A DEFENSE OF POETRY

The test of such poetry
is that it discomfits.

CHARLES BERNSTEIN

1   The lake trout is not a furious
    animal, for which I apologize
    that you have the mental
    capacity of the Anchovy.

2   Yes the greatest of your sister's
    facial pimples did outweigh a
    Turkey.

3   I was eating Vulture Beast
    Cream, I was eating Lippy
    Dung Corn, and I said "Your
    ugly dog is very ugly," for he is.

4   And that is when I turned and
    a snowflake banged into my
    eye like a rusty barge and I
    killed your gloomy dog with a
    mitten.

5   For I have bombed your cat
    and stabbed it. For I am the
    ambassador   of   this
    wheelbarrow and you are the
    janitor of a dandelion. Indeed,
    you are a teacher of great
    chickens, for you are from the
    town of Fat Blastoroma, O
    tawdry realtor. For I have
    clapped your dillywong in a
    sizeable door.

6   You have an achy knee, which is where I clubbed your achy and pompous knee. I shoot your buffalo, may you be hanged by the upper lip and somehow burned in a canoe.

7   Is your butt driving through traffic

that it should toot so at the world? I am averse to urine, yet I shake your hand upon occasion;

8   I have made a whiskey of your tears—and Joe-Bob made a flu-liqueur of your night-mucus;

9   That some of your gas has been banging around the market like a small soldier carrying a table. God booby.[1]

---

1.   Just as the fog is shackled to the dirty valley stream and cannot go out loosely to join the loopy clouds who contain hollering eagles and whooshing falcons but must stand low and bound and suffer the scratch of a bush and the round poop of deer and the odd black spoor of the American black bear or the bump of a car on a road or the sick crashes of paintings thrown from a rural porch, so also is your mind bound to the low reach of trash and the wet wan game of worms and the dripping dick of a torpid dog—and unlike the clouds above you you do not feel swell but clammy and pokey and sweaty: a

10   I overlook your titties. Your
      sneeze erased the blackboard
      and your cough knocked a dog
      into loneliness;

11   For you remind me of a dog
      hurled   over   a   roof—
      yapping to no effect. And
      furthermore   the   habitual
      peristalsis   in   your   bowels
      sounds like a barfight in a
      whale. In addition, that as a
      boy you lassoed storks with a
      petty friend named Jerry.

12   And just as you swallowed a
      cherry's stone and produced a
      tree, you recently ate a burger
      and found a bull honking
      among your feces.

13   For I would more expect a
      Pigeon to tote a rifle

14   than a wise syllable issue from
      your cheesepipe.

15   And as your nose is packed
      with Error, I advise you to pick
      it often.

---

leaf-smell follows you, odd breezes
juke your brook-chaff, lambs and
rachel-bugs go up and forth in you,
and when a car passes through you,
windows down, the car-pillows in
that car get puffy, absorbing water in
the air, and those pillows become
bosoms, gaseous moving bosoms,
and that is the nearest you come to
bosoms.

16   For you are a buttock.

      Indeed you are the balls of the
      bullock and the calls of the
      peacock; you are the pony in
      the paddock near the bullock
      and the peacock; you are the
      futtock on the keel and the
      fetlock (or the heel) of the
      pony in the paddock:

17   Indeed you are the burdock on
      the fetlock and the beetle on
      the burdock and the mite on
      the beetle on the burdock on
      the fetlock of the pony in the
      paddock and the padlock of
      the gate of the paddock of the
      bullock and the peacock.

18   Thus with you I am fed up.
      For you are Prufrock and I am
      Wild   Bill   Hickok   at   a
      roadblock with the wind in my
      forelock and a bullet in my
      flintlock. You are Watson I am
      Sherlock.

19   For you are the hillock and I
      am the hill; I am Hitchcock, O
      Buttock. You—are Cecil B.
      DeMille.

20   Yes he has thrown a squirrel at
      me   which   came   flapping
      through   the   air   like   a
      disjointed hairbrush.

21   The fact that the sequins on your dress caused you to look like the instrument panel of an airliner during a three-engine flame-out did not escape anyone's attention;

22   That your heart is a colostomy bag[2] and your brain is the Peanut of Abomination.[3] And that the cake frosting you just ate is actually earwax.

23   And since suing you would be like suing a squirrel, and since I would rather eat a mixture of powdered mummy and water than talk with you again,[4] I

---

2.   For these reasons and more, Dolores rightly asked as you walked by, "What is that smell that smells so much it is audible, is it a spoor?" I said it is the smell of a dillywong slammed in a door.

3.   Or the Dingleberry of Reason.

4.   Some have called your mouth Bippy-Swingset, and someone who seemed to resemble your physician called the orifice in question the birth-hole of a Raven, whereas it is common knowledge all Ravens are born in burning forests, for the beast is a charred contraption, being well-cooked and near dead. Some say that Crows are born out of a sail's white leeward wall, others that thun Crow is as an millet-corporal to the Raven's brook-colonel, that a pelican has goiter and that a Crow is in truth the silhouette of a gull knocked loose from that gull, which can happen in the case of an Sudden Explosion, where, in the afterclap

will try to punch your head
hard enough[5] that you will not
dare chase me, but not so hard
that others will hunt me.

24   For you have killed my family[6]
and I have killed your dog,
your bird, and the mouse of
your daughter;

25   Your cousins Rosie, Yolanda,
Amelia, Harriet, Johanna, and
Carol   have   all   been
decapitated.

---

and initial desolation, gulls will
breach the sky with such celerity
their silhouettes break free and fall
like dark packs to the ground, which
is why the Crow is a kind of angry
bird, being now without grace and
having a charred voice. Some insist
the Crow is in fact a drunk, though
at which saloon he find his beer or
how he should pay for it, or whether
he have beer, port, or an highball,
these "poets" will not aver: either
way he follows not the Doctrine of
Christ   and   is   a   derisive   and
condemnable   bird   and   ought
therefore to be avoided and never
frighten a gull. Another annoying
beast can be the Squirrel. For he is
midget blowhard.

5.   And like a pipe thrown at an eagle I
will send you folding to the humpy.

6.   I heard you once enquiring how you
were born and I told you then you
were created because your mother
subjected her privates to the
attentions of a bull. Which is why
you insist a cow says Ma when it is
clearly saying Moo.

26   But we pushed Judy over a cliff.[7]

---

7.   For: There was an Bee, who, flinging himself against his shadow in a Brooke, did drown, and so washed of his own Enmity, he did sail like a dark and brittle Bubble, to the general amphitheater of the Sea, where he was drowned a second time. Thus first he was sunk from Life and second from the Known; and now lies twice dead. Like this captious Bee, you will drop from the world and sink to oblivion.

ROBERT LOWELL

The great dog had broken his chain
and he chased my grandmother and me
a hundred yards
as if he were a people-hating cheetah.

We ran just past the oaken fence before grandmother farted
and sent the dog hurtling backward
in a blast of combed-away fur.

Her wind caught me in the nose and turned me like a rooster vane
and for a moment the world was in a fury.

Grandma was of course thrown forward
in the manner of a cuttlefish
who escapes by the explosion of ink.

It was her prerogative
to abandon me to face the dog alone
since she can't afford to be harried
by animals so late in life.

She gave no signal to me
before releasing her emergency burst,

but I was comforted by knowing she was now relaxing safe in her bulbous couch
as I stood in the pieces of her skirt
and readied myself to face
the fart-combed dog.

My uncles have a battle-brilliance
but I do not: I can't fight with only a hankie
or a little book. I need a log or a stanchion
from a charter boat: and right about then
I was wanting a long pole with a dog-impounder's hook.

I once inserted a baroque vase in the nostril of a cow
but I had nothing like that on hand today.

Running would have done no good as it was a fast dog and had already begun
        its pre-charge growl.

I had one of those small flags on a toothpick pole in my shirt pocket,
about the size of a piña-colada umbrella.

My plan was to Iwo Jima the flag into the body of the dog as it leapt at me.
I longed for a chopstick.

It finally charged and like the injured animal
it now was he fell dead with the flag in the marshland
of his right eye. The squirrels were rejoicing.

The ancient orange cat named Bill, its neck distended and jaw open in disbelief,
strode out of McIlveny's grand porch

and with the dexterity of a monkey
began to bat the dog
up and down the length of its body
as if testing a new xylophone.

By turns the cat looked furious and then content.
And there settled a kind of crappy, post-evil stillness
punctuated only
by the small thumps of McIlveny's cat.

And that cat seemed to be weeping in its anger at the dog.
And of a sudden I saw something of that cat in me

and wanted to scream and wave him out of there:

For I pitied it all that I had not yet learned
to avoid such scenes
with a blast of hot and backward air.

RICHARD WILBUR

When I question the world of myth and absolution
and consider, following one bent path of thought,
whether a pumpkin is a Catholic or a Lutheran
or down what tossed hall of tree and weed
the bunny went before it stopped,
    then I start and know
    how great old Richard Wilbur was.

What ceremony of light played with Sabrina
    in his mind! Is he dead yet? Is it night?
    Ho-hum: Wilbur
    was a quilter brave—bollufresco
of the verbal wind, quartz-smith
    of assonantal jade.

    Richard Wilbur, you are my mind!
The conscientious captains of my closet
where I store my heart-coat
    and my cap of hate
will not bring out, for me to wear,
the raincoat of my pout, the hunting hat
of my despair.
    It is because

I have been reading you of late.

Sometimes I fiddle with my groin, engage
with a sensibleness, mark menus, and generally steer
a path for goodness. And, too, at times,
    when my wife is sadly queer
or when a friend says something odd
I consider, Richard Wilbur, your stately verse
    and, generally, *thank God*. For God is great.

I know this because

I have been reading you of late.

DEAR HOUSEFLY

Today I whacked you, fly, who was making more fuss than
a ratty Volkswagen ascending a mountain:
I crushed you with the catechism of Augustine

(the German edition by Gustav Krüger,
which I'll wager
few have read, or will ever . . .):

thus *De Catechizandis Rudibus*
has pressed out your worried buzz, brought you
to a thimble-fountain of maggot pus.

And had I sent you off to Paradise, odd fly out of Hadrumetum,
had you been, say, a disciple of Chrysostom,

or a little optimist following Origen, rather than
a broom-chased peregrine, I might have let you go.

But there you were
just back from bugging mules, Gaul-blown,

smaller than the small books of Hippo.
What a life you must have had,

swirled in the breath of running dogs,
your eyes domed and numerous

as the basilicas of Carthage.

Sincerely,

Gabriel Gudding

POEM IMPLORING THE RETURN OF MY BUTT

Dear Sir—I have lost my butt. It was a
frail butt not unlike a dog's. Now
that it is gone I am concerned
about its recovery as my legs are
grating against my abdomen.

Sincerely,

Gabriel Gudding

INFANTRY

To Ken Burns

My Dearest Beloved Mommy, I have only one diaper left, provisions are running low, yet I will continue ahead with these onerous puddles and snows, until I make General McClelland's camp.

He is a big meany but I must rely on him in your absence to feed and nurture me. Mommy, I need cuddles and fear I will get none of your milk in McClelland's camp. Have you sent it on ahead?

Yesterday I thought I heard your burping and met a brutal man who pinches me. I crawled away from him last night into some pine barrens. For several hours today as I crept along the trail I was tormented by a bumblebee who poked and fizzled in my hair.

Mommy, please send your milk to General McClelland's camp. Send it care of

Gen'l McClelland
Beater-Upper, Mississippi

I will be there in a few days. I am tired and maybe send someone to carry me, any nanny or uncle. Yesterday a male dog tried to mount me. In the clouds this forenoon, I thought I saw a dolphin smiling. She was spouting a sandy milk from the old teat on her back—and making for some sunlight in the shore stones.

FOUNDRY

The great brass bell was dragging itself across a landscape mottled with parks and cricks and creased with old asphalt roads, its swollen clacker pathetically donking against the fire hydrants and curbs.

What had sent it packing? Was it going home? Fleeing a fired past?

Who had freed it from its weather-wracked, hulking cross-stays?

Once, the bell was caught in bracken like a large smooth bug in tar, a wheezing dog came fumbling, oddly didn't pee, just lay down beneath it and died. That smell of dog lingered in the bell's clacker swivel, repulsing cats for some time.

The winters were the worst; its big tired mouth dragging across the dirty snow like an early morning kiss.

Then, struck by a dump truck, it tottered on its lip for a moment. Until, like a humpbacked penny, it began that addled circuitous fall common to all coins, and lay still. The bell
was paralyzed.

It wasn't until dark and bluest winter that the shadow of a steeple was able to reach the bell, giving one reassuring stroke each day—until evil spring beat back the steeple's soft, compassionate arm.

ORCHARD

Just beyond a large basswood copse outside Moorhead, Minnesota, an immensely stupid man named Andersen had buried one end of an antler in the soil of the Red River Valley, hoping to grow a deer. That fall he looked down and saw a buck huffing in the garden plot, buried to its neck, its great chest breasting the soil. Andersen blurted oh-ohs and ha-has, the alarmed deer struggled to get out, humphing and oomphing. Soon Andersen had an expansive orchard of deer.

The deer in his orchard all faced one way. They stood at attention, always, the deer—as do children when a teacher barges through a door. They were as porpoises cresting a buried delta, each antler a stiff, ligneous spout—the knots of bone-pine rising from some blowhole deep in the fur and lodged on the skull bone. At times in the fog they resembled overlarge chickens or chihuahuas with bailing-wire hairdos; sometimes in the dragonflies, they seemed gull-honked frigates, and always, though, their buried chests were oaken casks, the tension in them aging.

Now, the skin of a porpoise is made of vegetal matter and not meat matter; and, just so, is the antler of deer not bone but wood matter. For a buck at his head is half tree, whereas only at the hips is he a creature who defecates. Of course we know that bushes and trees do not dung. Neither does a weed fuck nor a burdock kiss. Nor will a grape dismiss a comrade with a shrug or turn sternly on its vine and commend the vintner on cultivating its rubicund friends. No, the shrub dares not poop lest she be considered a nuisance and disposed of. Furthermore, were I a shrub I would not dung, as a shrub is incapable of moving away from its feces. Defecation is really an activity for mobile creatures. And so these deer, being fastidious and stationary, refused to defecate, their faces set hard with the strain of refusal,

until they eventually exploded, Andersen weeping, one af-
ter another, deer upon deer detonating, like so many domes
on a field of bubble wrap.

very little has been written. Moored to the ploppy mud by a languid mind, the bird is strapped to its tube of paste by a frail girdle. Having not much brawn, and being rickety in its construction, it is a kind of wicker bird. The rectum of a Peacock is thus like a flask in a picnic basket, as it might fall out if the bird is jostled. In this sense the Peacock's rectum is a fender on an ancient car: it sits at the back and rattles. If one kicks a Peacock, it is not unusual to knock the rectum clear out of the bird.

Peacocks have one rectum in common which they pass among them from Peacock to Peacock like a relay baton. Some people think that talent is like that. But it isn't: talent is not like the butt-baton of Peacocks. Any community has a surplus of talent and is unlike the community of Peacocks, which has an insufficiency of rectums.

The anus is a kind of larynx of the nether region: it is the only vocal cord unattached to the lungs. As such, it is an "independent" vocal cord—a kind of "colony" among vocal cords—a settlement of the voice in one of the body's distant regions. The rectum, for instance, is the rec room of the body, where our feces romp as children before entering the world. There is a certain amount of pomp at their graduation.

Each rectum is highly personal. Whereas a colostomy bag is a much more public device inasmuch as it hangs outside the body. A dog's rear end is public, but a human one is not. Insofar as the anus will allow light into the rectum during a fart, the rectum is a kind of camera obscura. Diarrhea, before it is released from the body, is like an annoyed Raven in a leather jar. Once I tried to kill a Walleye after a large dinner, but I had grown so fat at table that I had to relearn how to punch, and I felt like Humpty Dumpty trying to learn kung fu. My rectum became essential to my weight loss.

In the center of even the best display, is a little jumble of mush essential to the survival of said display. Once when a boy, I saw my mother's vulva reflected in a puddle. And do we all not come from puddles, waddling out with clapboard plumage—and eyes to be seen?

POEMS

I pick the chickadees off the bush sadly,
one by one. It is like picking berries
they are alive and happy chickadees,
bright fruits, song hens, they are
the lint of a rainbow.

I put them in my pockets. I put
one of the chickadees in my
bellybutton. I have stretched my bellybutton
to accommodate the chickadee. I have become
a marsupial. Sometimes, if we want,
we can carry a chickadee in our torso
like a colostomy bag of song.

SMALLTOWN FAUX PAS AMONG THE LEMONBARS

No one knows how the moonbeam cracked into the housecat
with the force of a plummeting log,

Or why the perfectly calm young woman chose to crush a roach so large
        that when she crushed it
        it made the sound of a heavy door falling into an old corn field.

And I fully concede that if anyone remembers anymore why under two summers'
        dust
        the smacked watch rests
        on top of the old armoire,
        they are not present to inform us.

        But it was certainly evident indeed to everyone that longest afternoon,
        including my emotionally injured mother and my lazy and feeble father
        —and including to my shame even my oldest grandmother,
        and my once gorgeous cousin who was now fat and gorgeous,
        (herself almost lost in dimming senility)—
        and my dim uncles could see it too, everyone young and old could see

        why I did not make the requisite euphonious sounds about the simple quilts
        to the old churchladies
        while we ate the lemonbars
        in the cool half-forgotten church basement
        on that otherwise most insignificant Sunday.

THE PALLBEARER RACES

It is morning in late summer.
I am moving in the yard at the Church of Our Redeemer,
which hangs at the hems of two flax farms, a mile
on the highway from the edge of Flom.

Near the picket gate, in the weeds grown up
into the chipped paint, our family's disinterred
rest there with the flies, beside my comely aunts
gussied in pitch.

Their cheeks are gemmed with tears
lit pink in the coming sun, itself lately exhumed
and fresh as Christ: today the pallbearer heats
at Our Redeemer church. And I, by God,
am taking bets.

Every ten years we've dug them up
and the men of the family have grunted them
to the edge of Thompsen's shorn field and back,
in a race whose purpose is, for a day at least,
to give our grief a shallow grave.

And though a year gone
and mostly bone,
little Tom will race today, carried by James and Jake
and Bill and Dave and John—
and one other whom I don't know.

He'll do fine. They slide him now
from the Fleetwood's bed,
shoulder him with a huff, and walk—
his aggregate clicking in the box.

The last hearse arrives
popping over the gravel.
The churchyard pauses

while we put Raymond near the gate.
The wind bellies thick
in the shadows near my aunts,
as one of Ray's sisters begins to keen
and another to ululate.

And beyond the headstones,
as if remembering the days when she could run
an old mother toes the starting line
at the back of the churchyard lawn.

I shall root for Tom.

BAIL

Discussing farm prices through the fields, we came upon the haybale in the afternoon as the storm broke open, and my father claimed, God knows why, that I had not done this or that.

As we continued the argument he had started, I saw how little education he had.

Something swam up from the depths to his eyes—an old thought, from the look of it, a battered green carp that had prudently stayed at the bottom of some fetid lake in him, and had rarely seen light—but all it made was a slight watery splutter at his lips, when it flashed away and was gone again.

At which point I sought to instruct my father on his character in the hope I could again draw up to his face the vert and squamous beast, that I might exorcise the animal by beating my father about the eyes.

We argued for some time. And though it appeared a small distracted fish, I could see, on occasion, its shadow swim close to his face, until, almost surfacing in his expressions, it would descend again. I could see also, far out on that lake in his eyes, a good man in an average boat bailing water slowly as it rained. Every so often I would raise my fist as we argued. And put it down again. As a good man in him bailed.

RONALD REAGAN

Where are all the lost
and discarded
teddybears gone?

Where did those
worn butlers
in the house of
Innocence go?

Are they now cast low among card games
in some lawless
closet land,
Nancy?

Has something bad befallen
Patched Old Holmes and
Bunny Jake, hapless
beyond the davenport,
far over the
      back of the
blank divan?

I tell you
they are playing banjos
and living in messy rooms
far past the cardigans,
beyond the little country band
of hobo
flipflops: safe
from those Sandinista
rag dolls.
They are living in a
post-Communist state,
Nancy.

They don't mourn for the death of
JFK or
M
LK. The
flies in their rooms
are only wafted yarn-snarl; outside,
in the pillow-cuffed weather, a gull doily zings and
dang if that's not a hurly bean-bag on the ecliptic
being the sun, O
the world is heavy for beings
who were so long carried,
Nancy.

THE PARENTHESIS INSERTS ITSELF INTO THE TRANSCRIPTS OF THE COMMITTEE ON UN-AMERICAN ACTIVITIES

"Senator (I have never lain with rubrics,
nor am I among the indicted's
swart date books: I am the anchorite's
punched lips. Small-lunged boys
who duck in the old beds from dogs
have lain low in me;
rabbits, I think, have bolted here
who smell a cold hole
in the fuck-all blurry middle
of a life sprint. The ant
comes to me for its mortar: I am the divots of the
ballpeens, cane marks
outside libraries. I fell from a tree planted on a hill
of the earth's early ticker tape; I cracked open,
a walnut of ticker tape. I am a tick
in the hide of the book, seed
of the monograph: Yesterday the dewpoint fell
and a big fog issued from the comma—meadows
in the semicolons filled with tractors, the plow's tines
are made of me, as were the eyelashes of Elijah, fingernail moons
of Coltrane—my heelmarks
are scattered in the mesquite tree, I was abused
by cummings.
The day the pennies pitched their tents
on the banks of the math books,
I became their tent stakes. Queens
have walked in me for I am smoother
than a dashboard: Jerusalem
is just this booth in the heat, but I'm
the backrooms of Nineveh, cowry's arcature. I respect the oyster
for being the grotto of a single mood—but in me
a canyon's filled with stones
sweetly immobile, in me an old man's laundry
sculls on the slantlight. I am a small girl's middle, suitcase

of the vivid poor—farthest cousin
of a thistle's tribe, having struck and hung on
    in this most drifting soil: my whole family was born
  in an un-neutral footnote
and was taken out into the wire and weeds
    and shot in the gravel; it is on gravestones that I am
      the cradle of years,
        and) I have to say
   it's a pleasure
    to appear before you
      in this honored room."

BOSUN

He of all can reeve a rope best.
"THE SOLDIER," HOPKINS

In that first winter week across Alaska's gulf
The chain's cold bell clacked on its locked gear:
Its anchor knocked imploring on the hull.

He trained me twelve-hour days in the sea's ratcheting air,
Under a sky grey and empty as a dead brain.
I tried to keep my food, but his slick toothed sneer

Drew up bacon, then bile, then lunch and bile again,
As if his task was to see what I would bear.
Heartless, he saved my bow-work for open water,

Said, "Keep your ass to the bitts, you fucking crumb,"
And gruffed I whip 400 feet of hawser.
Blisters rose in my hands like curdled cream.

My ass sank and copped air as the bows
Bit green water, swallowed, and rose up to spit.
Two days I sat there and whipped—twenty hours,

Wedged in the cusping stem like a limpet.
I could see him sometimes leering in the wheelhouse window,
And all I could hear, through my mantra not to quit,

Was the anchor's sodden gonging through the fo'c's'le.
Never had I worked so hard just to sit
In one place, that wet, for such an asshole.

The bosun watched my every move—
His eyes screwed an impatient expertise
Into my slack job, taught me how best to drive

The marlinspike and fid, to sog the grease
Through the high rigging, haul the guys
Without tearing delts—to do it with ease.

I remember now how the weird ripping of wind through wind
Scalloped the water over the pitted deck,
Fingered my hair, and went frothing into the tarpaulin

Like God rifling through the things he's made.
I can still see the lenient Boston captain,
Ray-Bans of the whiskery, ursine mate;

Can recall the cook's bullet-struck head, tone
Of Jew-hate murder in the oiler. I can recite
The punch-lipped words of the bosun's ragging,

And remember the sleet tossed twice, the let-loose barrels;
I'll even name the forepumps and valves above them:
But what I do *not* remember precisely

Is how the bosun made me love him.

TO AN OKLAHOMA IN WINTER

Thy trills of shrieks by rocks and hills return'd
"TO A LOCOMOTIVE IN WINTER," WHITMAN

You for the cavalry recidivist
For the Trail of Tears; you for the late "thy"—thy
        mudwell capitol, your
        colored fountain

You for the angry panhandle
        in the kitchen of the Confederacy
For your Jiffy Pop over Texas

For your sturdy, wearing wind, the bloody ankle
        cracked on ice. You for the old squaw
        with the wrong thigh. In your malady and hate, your groom
    of summer, mother and child

You in the abandonment, oil and corn, Will Rogers
        and bobcat, your loud civet
under rubble of midnight. You
in the mines and wild turkey: the drunk
and stuporous thieves, your duck-bonked
rivers, man-kicked brides your lead, your short tons
        your Creeks and Chickasaws

        Cherokees and Choctaws your Seminoles
        and Federal Supervision

For your displacement

For the beaver and plover and swan
        shot in the hips
for your highways your hard dawn
        for your heartland

and Edward P. Murrah
for your fat dam on the Pensacola and Verdigris
your Tenkiller Ferry
for your grim wine stuffed with mung beans
your weird-headed murderess those half-wits
your coalman peppered at noon
Custer and Kiowa your Greer your seacloud skewered
over Ellis Okfuskee Adair

for your Pawnee out loose, the bristles
over Nowata: your Craig, and Delaware
        for the Ottawa: your deforestation, your
        mental health, your "pacification"
of the Quapaw the Osage your hell
        from Arkansas the federal ankles, your trashdump
of Jackson, the butted Wichita; Your torture
in rain, your rape
        in corn: your Yankee rapine, your Union rapine,

        for the broken-backed bin of children, the extended
        hole and bin:

        for your Iowa, Oto and Kickapoo. Thee
for the death of the Arapaho.

You
        for the truckbomb exonerating.

ONE PETITION LOFTED INTO THE GINKGOS

For the train-wrecked, the puck-struck,
the viciously punched,
　　　the pole-vaulter whose pole
　　　　　　snapped in ascent.
　　　　　　　　For his asphalt-face,
his capped-off scream, God bless
　　　his dad in the stands.
　　　　　　　　For the living dog in the median
car-struck and shuddering
　　　　　　on crumpled haunches, eyes
　　　　　　　　wide as gates, seeing nothing, but looking
looking. For the blessed pigeon
who threw herself from the cliff
　　　　　　after plucking out her feathers
　　　　　　　　just to feel what it's like to fall. For
the poisoned, scalded and gassed, the bayoneted,
　　　　　　bit and blindsided,
　　　　　　　　asthmatic veteran
who just before his first date in years and years
swallowed his own glass eye. For these and all
and all the drunk,

Imagine a handful of quarters chucked up at sunset,

lofted into the ginkgos—
　　　　　　and there, at apogee,
　　　　　　　　while the whole ringing wad
pauses, pink-lit,
　　　　　　about to seed the penny-colored earth
　　　　　　　　with an hour's wages—
As shining, ringing, brief, and cheap
　　　　　　as a prayer should be—

Imagine it all falling

into some dark machine
        brimming with nurses,
            nutrices ex machina—

and they blustering out
        with juices and gauze, peaches and brushes,
to patch such dents and wounds.

THE LYRIC

I

had an oven of gladness
in which I baked
days of boo-hoo and sadness.

I baked the days of boo-hoo
into crusts of fuck-it.

I had tried to bake my woe-dough to wow-bread.
But lacking the mojo or know-how
to turn my woe-dough to wow-buns,

all I could do
was bake my days of boo-hoo
into crusts of fuck-it.

WISH

I will drive down the gravel roads of my heart
back into my fucking childhood
until the roads are boulder roads, and I
am stuck again in the gigantic country
of being short.

Then I will dismount my heart-car
and walk the shore of the old familiar lakes
hoping to see my grandfather again
who used to fly kites with me
in the Athabascan wind.

YOUTH OF THE BACKHOE

I was a sundial. But I had an hourglass figure. And my husband
  was the second fountain pen of Edward R. Murrow.

And I tell you I was the brother of an oil derrick,
  the father of four catapults;
    was befriended by a truck and betrayed,
      jackhammered into twenty churchbells.

& Lord knows I was the lover of a metric wrench,
  whereas my nuts were standard.

And though I was a henhouse, a kettle drum, a buoy in a shallow bay,
and an aileron, at least I was a jubilant & a patient demon
  got up in metal & in love
  with the peppermint sun

before my teeth cut
the first loam at dawn.

MEMOIRS OF THE BACKHOE

"It's iron. And iron don't give a shit."
CAPTAIN BILL PETERSEN, APRIL 4, 1992,
SOMEWHERE IN THE GULF OF ALASKA

Once in Yellowstone
I watched a beaver launched cooked
from that one fastidious geyser.
        The thud was holy.

I recall the cold hanks of nylon hawsers strewing the foredecks on the glabrous
        waters
                of Frederick Sound.

I recall the shots from the fantail. Our wake sewn with albatross.

I recall the tired belligerence of Tyrone Tremblay who died crushed on a gravel
        berm
after a 30 foot flight on his *Husqvarna 400*.
His belt buckle ignited the gas tank.
His jacket burned for 40 minutes.

Once, on a dark day, the sun bobbed in oily clouds
like a cheap green apple, & all it did all day
was shine & roll, shine & roll.

It was in that old man's demesne, in a rake-littered yard, beached on cinder blocks
        that I feared to come to rest—and have. My treads are bobbysox.

I ate cake with the Prince of Dahomey & ran strewing my clothes through his
        cornfields
                chasing his daughter.

I drank the coldest *Kirschwasser* with my friend Christian Krogstad
                before he became a snob.

I recall the brooding doodles dark as fudge drawn by Joseph Stalin at Yalta—
                or something like them in the purple midden
                of the Woodland abattoir.

And only today my treads were clanking like colossal tumblers of Chardonnay
toasting all that had been buried under corn & sunlight
before the foreman jiggled my gears like the wind in a rosebush
and tapped away my glimmer and crash.

I tell you, it seems like months that my bucket was wind-shook above the grass.

AFTER YEATS

When I am old and using Revlon hair dye
and am sucking up my pharmacopoeia,
and can drink but Sanka—
when I don't have too many friends anymore
and the bathroom is a place of loneliness—

Yes, when I am old and Revloned and hypnogogic
and nodding at the wheel,
take down this book
and read of one who phoned you less and less,
but who dug you and remembered
your elegant hand
and somewhat geeky look.

THE *OED*

for Mairéad

It wasn't just that she was hot. It's that she was hotter
        than the frothing toe paint of the shining Maid of Orleans
the night her mare & she were martyred.
I guess it was just that she was far swankier
        than Joan the night of July seventeenth
        (14 Hundred 30), when she was anointed at Rheims.

Which is considerably swanky, for
only eight & sixty nightfalls later
they jarred Joan's ashes & hucked them in the water,
        & her palaver is drowned now in the Seine's.
I thought she was *that* hot. Maybe hotter.
I was red-faced as a robbed crab when I first saw her,
boiled & twirled in his froth-ripped pot.

I dreamed I thumbed her large big toe
        (large & larger in my palm)
& nipped the nail & smoothed the aequor
(whose door-stopping growth I could hear even then—
a low, a muffled vowel,
sub rosa—glacial.)
I wanted to say to her,
        "The whole of you, the mobile all—
        from your tintinnabular
        ears to your bumbinate growl,
        from your fricatives to your pianissimo—
really gets me. I mean *Really*.
        [I would say all of this while still holding her toe.]
        You are edible, considerable: *e.g.*
I've never seen a mastoid like yours;
It's quite a bone. Your hair was made for men-at-arms—
I'll be your horsey, and you could be my Joan."

But I realized spouting this would not be smart—or
even funny,
since Joan of Arc was cooked for being Joan of Arc.
     (But the moniker frankly fit her,
        for she was that hot—or maybe hotter.)
(I was addled) Instead I only said "Hello: ah, Hello there, Honey"
     and then skedaddled—said I had to check an *O-E-D*
(something about a 2 syllable Inuit word for
blood-flecked snow, ending in "brōn.")
     She thought *I* was odd. But she was odder.

DAYBOOK TO OYSTER, HIS INFANT DAUGHTER

for my daughter Clio

Too bad that heavy dime, the sun, can't fall
and crack the cope of your armored mouth,
plunk through the cakey sea, slamming conchs,

and turn the entire shebang
black and cold as you: leave you free
in a fried and indigent sea.

Maybe then you'd tell me what it's like
to be born beyond desks, nudger, poor-born Siamese twin
of the shovel.

But I'll wait for what you *will* say,
eons from now, how you'll tell me again
of an umbral summer,

sunlight stuck in the clay at the bottom-end
of pools, your heart
a chilly worm—a small, compulsive gourmand—

I'll say, I understand, I
was young once too and fruit
blew through my eyes; such a big jargon

and wonder were before me
that I heard my own heart banging
like a lost cart through

the summer's giant district
or the summer like a cart itself
lumbering in its oxenness, its own wool and oil.

I'll ask, What crunches burst around you, the water
turning it to tiny rumbles?—the depth charges, Titanics, the jackstays,
columnar sunlight bristling with tire irons?

I'll want your opinion
on the brisk refrigeration of the wind
flapping its broad laundry, the arrogant, tumbling cotton

of the whitecaps, gull-get light shining
its high Republican flag,
and how it was in the plumbate murk

napping with sinkers, vast trash, the unguent silk
in the drift-bake of diatoms. I'll want to know
how you got on

under the long escutcheon of delicious water
where the dark bricklayer lays her brick
keeping the yard:

down in the *Grundlage*
where the air-world's no louder
than the mouse-hiss of a match.

———

Such a practical family's up here
waiting for you: there are your sisters
—those porcelain saucers—

who've made the decision
to lay themselves out
for teacups and butter;

and your idiot brother still
would rather be nothing else
than a divot of asphalt. And I should tell you

that the dimwit axeheads thwunking the wood
are your lout-headed cousins, and the miniate adze
slapping the oak and linden

tipped off the ululant saw
of colonial America. Though what should you care
of the long and short of cutlery,

the west halls of the entrenching tool, the east
of the apple-spade, slick sink
of the scuffle hoe trepanning the chelsea loam

under the fescue—
or the song slung along a sunken pipe
when struck by the whack of the loy—

these are all the facts, familial and dry,
of mud and wood, and the general bother
of an arid world. You've got it good

under all this hubbub.
When you become a book
I'll say There was such this tiny godlet

in your belly, a muscle so smooth
it was almost gone, so still
it took the ocean in its imperfect lung, and

coughed out this giant of a mild chuckle
from the tiny chunk of a thing you were—
I'll remind of *that*, at least.

And just to raise a laugh I'll say
you were the chiefest bosun of golfballs,
lost commander of marbles, stripped bolts, captain

of greased bearings
on the forgotten little cars,
a sea-sergeant of axles—fine herdsman

of wave-flogged flotsam:
that you were *just* toward the shaggy
misoriented tribes

among your toys.

ADOLESCENCE

The duck is attacking Humpty Dumpty. She
    is brutalizing him.

They are filling up the oasis with shouts.

Realizing he must fight for his life,
    Humpty begins to roll vigorously
    about the sand dunes, attempting to knock the duck over.

Every so often the egg stops rolling, gets
    his bearing, beats his chest fiercely
    (but not so hard as to crack himself)
    and starts rolling again,
    trying to knock the duck over.

Of a sudden, Humpty stops
    and shrieks, "Mother?!
    Is that you?"

For who would have considered what kind of egg
    was Humpty Dumpty?
    I always assumed large chicken
    goose, once I thought, "Oh he's
    pterodactyl f'r sure."
    But never, "Duck."

"Mom! It's you, isn't it!"

And as the duck fumbled for an appropriate response,
    and just as Humpty was gathering himself
    so that he could articulate

his rage and confusion and resentment
    at his mother's behavior,

a duckling's head burst through Humpty's shell at his shoulder.

Albumen was everywhere.

Then the duckling's snot head periscoped
around and dumped its beak into the pot of Humpty's head.

And kicking the bottom out of him, the duckling finally orgasmed
itself from the warm shards and faced its mom. And the mother,

in an arpeggio of duck noise,
ran to embrace
her true child.

PEDAGOGY

for Marina

I guess I was going on in a rather good,
                    somewhat brilliant rattle
about the folding of the present indicative active
                    into the gerund or the gerundive
                    (or was it the general verbal adjectival?),
when I looked up from my spot of table—
                    which was quietly bearing the weight
                    of an ever growing doodle
                scored deeply as if in granite
                                    or maybe in marble
                by my ever more distant right hand—

& saw that all gathered there & listening
                    were like unto England's marsh birds
                    in a strong marsh wind—
                that is to say, they had the look of the dithered,
                                    or the bothered,
                                    but not the bedazzled;

and this was off-putting, if not place-putting,
                    & my right foot began pat-patting,
                    my ever more distant right foot,
                        pat-patting under the table
                    "like a sage escaped
                    from the inanity of life's battle."

        So: above the table, a saltmarsh of birds, & beyond them
                    the bird-stitched beach, breakers'
                muffled tympani
                        (& the long-lunged
                            bush-curled
                                smell of myrtle),
        &, under,
                the little sage tapping on; while, over
                    —& on—the table

a three pound doodle—
and before everyone a doodle,
& above every doodle
a pencil—
            & two eyes fixed, bunny-dazed,
on the lead of each pencil,
            as under the pencil trailed a trail of lead
drawn wearily from the pencil wood
            by the penciled paper, much as the sky would
            in drawing the thin jet vapor
            from a cold speck of jet
                in the worn sky air—

& each of these doodles must have weighed
            as much as a boiled egg or maybe an onion,
                though one looked like the moustache of Stalin,
                    & another like Stalin's hair,
            & one maybe like a velvet cushion,
                    an ancient cushion sold, say,
                by Sotheby's in London:

And I realized, after a long, or rather a distended, second,
        that I was living
        in the paradise of Horace Mann
                (of olden Massachusetts)
        or, more precisely,
                Johannes Comenius,
                as outlined in
                Pansophiae Prodromus,

        that in fact grammar and pencils, or pencils alone
                would never be fun again,
        that I ought to maybe thus
                light out for the margins
        or maybe the Everglades
                or maybe my alma mater, Evergreen,
                and be as a coin going plinkety,
        that I should do this early now-now,
                before the blicky hair-bird

49

bursts hard from my doodle—as a coin going plinkety—
and devours my middle section, inclusive of my ding-dong,
    do this now-now,
          and they WILL say O-O
          who IS that that goeth from Edom,
       with dyed garments from Bozrah? traveling
       in the greatness of his strength-O?

POEM ABOUT MY STRABISMUS

for Robert Duncan

If eyes are the windows of the soul, mine are bay windows.
Sometimes my eyeballs begin clubbing each other with paddles.
When the adults told me as a child to look both ways before I crossed the road
I could do it without turning my head.

I think I am crosseyed because my eyeballs are trying to see up my nose's skirt.
But with my fingers I have lifted up the flap of either nostril
to show my eyes there is no vulva in my nares. A porpoise swam by

and my right eyeball punched it in the blowhole.

I saw the dog running from me
and my left eyeball gave it a good slug in the rectum.

It is a gruesome memory to recall my very sight being flung at a beagle's end.

Eyeballs may be the gonads of one's forehead—
Why else do we say "eye balls" unless "testicles of the face"?

When will my head fly off my body?
        When my sight-wings untangle:
You will see it out there in the field eating acorns
and shitting oaks from its throat.

CHANGEABLE HEAD

Someone cut off my head and punted it.

In mid-flight the ears
turned to wings, the nose
became an anus, and the mouth remained a mouth.
But there was a beak on my forehead
and the handlebar moustache had turned to legs.

And this new bird
flew and roosted on a puppy,
frightening the puppy a great deal.

The guy who cut off my head
was now going to hitchhike with me, the torso,
into the sewer.

The head-bird tried to block the sewer
but it was kicked off again,
sailing away with a thump.

Having a rough time in the world, the head-bird
flew up and perched on a kite
that a little girl was flying.

It would be very
difficult to explain to
the little girl what was
perching on her kite.

I am telling this story from
the water purification plant
where I am caught in the filters
like a large dung.

For her part the little girl sees a
distant mobile pumpkin in the sky.

It is amazing what the wind can
    keep aloft.

COALMAN

> And Jesus saith unto him, The foxes have holes,
> and the birds of the air have nests; but the Son of
> man hath not where to lay his head.
> MATTHEW 8:20

in memory of Tom Andrews

I could have stayed up all night in my haversack,
in which I had devised to bivouac
just outside of Hackensack, New Jersey,
though I was wearing only a jersey
and was camping in a field of Guernseys or Jerseys.

I had lost my tent in Trenton. It was Lent again,
and I'd given up nothing less than comfort,
having decided to get to the heart of the matter.
Which I'd done well enough except
for the bottle of Southern Comfort

I'd kept to keep my sojourn warm and
help me read by the light of the Coleman lantern,
which I'd stolen hoboing from a coalman on a coal car just south of Boston
as I was barreling northward one summer
on a Burlington Northern.

The coalman saw me grab the Coleman from the coal car,
and I ranneth for cover and he ran after:
thus we both lit aftward, faster and faster
bounding from coal car to coal car, steel car
to fuel car, car car to truck car

(that was the general pattern). The coalman
was cussing and coughing like a cowboy
and I knew it was either I make it to the caboose or it's the hoose-
gow for me. Well, I hit the back of the back car
just as he hit the front of it, and I leapt

and thought that was the end of it. But now,
recall that as we're lunging aftward and aftward,
no one's loading coal into the coal car's
boiler, which must have been low to begin with—
because as we're going faster and faster aftward, the train's

going slower and slower forward:
and by the time I'd reached the aft end—either the stern or the stem
as it might be called on the water—the train
was traveling the same speed in both directions: in other words
nowhere. I was in deep water

for I believe the coalman now felt at leisure
to chase me farther than the limits of his vessel: I ran southward
in the opposite direction of the great train's former direction of travel,
but by that time we'd passed through Boston
and were somewhere just north of it,

as well as just north of a railroad trestle,
onto which I ran like the devil,
for he was big, the coalman,
though not, thank God, as big as his shadow.
Which is to say it was late, very late,

and night was about to settle
over us—and I looked over my shoulder
and saw
that his eyes
were murderous. He ran

and I ran—by now far from the train
and far from the trestle,
pumping harder and harder, deeper
and deeper into a night darker
and darker: I ran

with the coalman chasing after. We splashed
through tunnels, whammed
across overpasses. I ran out
over the water of bridges, cranking
in my fear, crossed,

and cranked it out again. I saw cows
dimly among dark weeds, I was out
among the farthest rickety signs, my
bubble of light blasted over broken shacks,
old stations, over older and older

tracks at the backs of schoolbuses without tires, I ran
with the coalman chasing after:
I thought of my mother, I thought of my daughter—
I thought of my wife and my father as I ran
faster and faster, farther and farther, into a night

darker and darker:
I ran for the border
but there was no border. I ran for Boston
but was far north of it, I thought of my brother
but I had no brother.

So I wished for a brother, I wished hard and harder
for a brother who were as large or larger
than the coalman,
who as he ran seemed to grow taller and taller:
I wished the coalman

were anything but a murderous coalman:
why not a banker, a baker, a postman: why not
money or bread or mail
to weight him down thus.
I tried to holler

but I could not holler. Cats
came in that night and went, dogs
long and big crossed my path
and clipped off frightened, a horse
I saw

in the brief circle of light
but it faded clopping into ditches
as I flickered over miles and miles
of track: I needed water. I needed rest:
I needed rest and water. The night

was growing green
around us. It was almost dawn. A chill
was hinging overhead, and as
the light gained I switched off
the lantern: Morning

came fully then:
I looked back
and stopped: I would like to say that when I looked back
the coalman was gone.
But he wasn't:

I walked
and he walked: We walked
to Trenton,
where we fought a fight
out of Milton,

or maybe of Samson
and Delilah
on their wedding night,
or possibly of Samson
who pummeled the donkey to death with its own jawbone

or possibly when Samson
went to Timnath and beat up the moneychangers or the renters,
                or was it the lion he rent?
or when Samson caught the glorious foxes in Judges
and did not beat them, no,
Samson did not beat the foxes

he burnt them to death
in his neighbor's corn, the foxes wishing
they were somewhere in Leviticus,
that is how we fought, we fought
as if God were drawing us

in pencil
swiftly,
as if God
were furiously sketching
two brothers.

CHARGE OF THE L. B.

C'est magnifique mais ce n'est pas la guerre.
GENERAL BOSQUET

What padlock-sized toads I sent and stained
across the rain-terrible roads
      that skirt the sun's bloom so far now from Karlsbad.
      I have come through the valley of Belbek,

and my bullets pop-whack from the gallop
artfully, as if we—gun, horse,
      bullet and I—were of Vienna all, the music
      of a deadly Vienna. I have come

with skill and red-hot shot, hot
as the sun
      at 3 o'clock.
      I am innocent as a horse. Cubby-

hole-faced, I am an earl, Lord Cardigan, high putz
of Hussars.
      I shall kill the Crimean army with only
      this chicken bone. Then I will throw it

into the flesh-spangled wastes of Crimea
where it will circle like a boomerang
      beheading every child and woman
      east of the Bolga.

See Lord George, behind me in the charge,
sucking in, at trot, a lit cigar,
      that lasts him to the guns. Oh my Hussars:
      their coveralls tight as cherry skins

and that red, and what a pretty rose of fire bloomed
over Cranrobert's hill, though it smelled of bone:
      splinters of oaken cannon & horsen leg
      shot into the nearer air,

cumbrously the guns leveled on our chargers, and
into the trot, gait, and racking pace,
          minié ball flew and we took it all
          in the nets of our ribs.

And into our verve and almost groupie love
the whole chalked world of mineral flew
          toward our gadundering horses, bilious jaws, twirling
          flecks of ligaments, spattered fetlocks: nothing dry now:

Big teeth sprayed in prisms. Here and there a billiard-like eyeball
had lost its horse, everywhere
          the severed tails, pinging flick of knuckle-
          balling shrapnel, again the flogging whirl

and piebald smacks of shell, blood sponged deep
in pelisses of fur, & lots of bullion braid splattered filthy. Oh fuck me
          what glory! and all I said, God love me,
          when they

tried to break the trot and charge,
was "Steady! Steady the 17th Lancers!"
          and there was no long charge that day
          we *trotted*

through the valley of death. Trotted
through grape, great shot, volleys that plumed
          in gristle.
          But we would not hustle.

The Lancers, Dragoons, the Light Dragoons,
the 8th and 11th Hussars!
          There goes the hand of Shewell! flying back
          into the west!

There goes Beltel's head like a magnificent crow
flapping into the hoof-mud!
      Until finally the men, blast them, broke
      the canter,

and between the Fedioukine Hills and Causeway Heights
we cantered in reducing numbers
      toward the battery wall of smoke white booming
      where, tomorrow, the sun *will* rise. And Oh

at 80 yards we were all frightfully ready to kill, really,
And we charged,
      just so,
      into the guns.

FOR QUINTUS LABERIUS DURUS, WHO, BECAUSE OF A JAVELIN IN HIS LUNGS, DIED NEAR KENT, IN EARLY AUGUST, 54 B.C.

> If every man had a window in his breast . . . , or, that which
> Tully so much wished, [that] it were written in every man's
> forehead what he thought about the Republic . . . what a deal
> of laughter it would have afforded!
>
> ROBERT BURTON, *ANATOMY OF MELANCHOLY*

> *In eo die Quintus Laberius Durus, tribunus militum, interficitur.*
>
> JULIUS CAESAR, *DE BELLO GALLICO*

       Bored and nosing again in Caesar's *Gallic Wars*
and feeling arrogant as usual about knowing Latin,
I crossed one sentence in his dinky book
that was frankly sick: It read, "On that day, Quintus Laberius Durus,
tribune of soldiers, was killed," witnessing empty
as a newspaper stand: truncated, enduring,
more than bland. His single chronicler wrote
in martial prose—generous as a watercolorist—an epitaph
thin as shorebirds. Nothing else.
       Pissed off at Caesar
and sorry for Durus, I continued to nose, smelling out
for Quintus Laberius, tribune of soldiers.

They had weighed anchor off the kidney-beaned beach at Walmer,
and, at low tide, almost bored, after breakfast and their morning turd,
they donned armor with one resigning sigh just the instant the sun rose
out of the great blue-gray tulip of the North Sea. And when the choppy clouds
were hanging with that taffeta that they hang with at dawn,
they leapt into the black-ebbed slackwater, which, the scholars tell us,
was Caesar's bad idea, since the *milites* were forced to run knees high
in chest-deep channel water
for two hundred very unfunny yards, arrows
skipping in their faces, helmets
lit by the roosting dawn, running as soldiers
have always run: like baked cheese on legs or something.

Caesar ordered the low-draft galleys—his mean chihuahuas
of 'I mean business'—to hurl
his heaviest javelins, with their great winch-strung skeins of hair,
at the Celts of Cassivelaunus (who fight naked, Caesar
is fastidious to mention),
until the Celts backed off, flipping Caesar the bird with much asperity,
in their vast barbaric sign language. Their retreat
flickered with arrows like finches
flushed from burning elms. Darts and blood were everywhere.
It was a very pointy morning.

But this is not the day that Quintus Laberius Durus died.

Cassivelaunus' rabid flocks
followed Caesar a fortnight
picking at his army,
which elbowed inland forty miles,
whether chased or marching, he does not say—
he tells us only
eighty thousand paces.

(And if you imagine the men who had to count this out,
you will know
that of the seven soldiers ordered to tally, two
grew corns and five had feet
blistered so cruelly
they looked ripe
with cranberries. The soldiers
had all miscounted.)

And as some were squabbling
about the paces and whether they should tell the "Great Julius Caesar,"
whose temper matched his mercy, that they were somewhere between, oh,
twenty and forty miles, give or take,
from the beany stones of Walmer's berms
and their only longboats home—

as some were squabbling this way,
Caesar ordered fortifications, a rampart and trench,

pickets and posts and fences for livestock, and men
        to guard these operation,
        among whom, of all the men of Legion Ten,
        he assigned the tribune

Quintus Laberius Durus.
                Durus,
which means Hard.

And as Caesar was deciding where he was,
(which is a commander's privilege—
to simply *decide*
where you are),
and as his palisade was being erected,
the Celts of Cassivelaunus
threw themselves like stones
crashing from the wood
and attacked the *praeses* of Legion Ten,
praeses, which means
"those who sit in front." In front, that is,
of the walls.

It was on that day
that Quintus Laberius Durus, a tribune of soldiers, who sat before the walls,
died
before the eyes of Caesar, and his men.

Even Caesar remarked
that the popping sound of his chest
when the javelin struck
and punched daylight through him
was uncommon.

But for the soldier Quintus Laberius Durus who died near Kent,
I have no pity. That he met his pop-eyed end
beating helter from a great blue man
whose limed hair raged taut in the wind, drumlike as an umbrella
that is quickly opened in a car,
does not concern me.

That he once walked the ridge of battle at its peak,
cocky as a chimney cleaner, and as antique,
doesn't bother me, nor should it bother us: he was a soldier
and it's their job to die like this.

What bugs me
is that his last breath
                went through the air chuckling
                for his friends, without his wife, in a field he did not know,
                near some river they call the Thames,

                and lingered against the sky, winding with the herons,
warranting only
a nine word sentence.

FONS BELLI

Rummaging around in my anus
I pulled out
a tormentum and a robinet,
a petrary and a matafunda:

a fundibulum, a manganum, and a martinet.

Indeed I plucked out an engine-à-verge, a blida and a bricolé.

I plucked out a beugle, a fronda, a ballista and calabra.
All of these came out
with relative ease, they rather slid
as if on a sledge or a slide or a sleigh.

But it was the awful 50 foot trebuchet
—big enough
for throwing clowns and plows—
that gave me hella that day.

I'm sorry for these details
But that's how it was:

Thank God
for enemas.

TIPPETYCANOE DELENDUM EST

Tired of desks and counters and attentive stances,
of counters crossed with curses and of-courses
and of the supercilious appraising glances

of the clerks and Clarks and Shirleys and sheriffs
of the cake-like courthouse of our county courthouse,
of metermaid and bailiff,

                  I say

Let me be blithe in dealing with the world—

                But not today

        when I go into
        the Tippetycanoe County Courtyhouse
          to set matters right,
             clacketing
             with the metal
             of military Jehosaphat.

     There the cops look of the freeway and are numbered
           three and thirty,
     there the cops are booking and booted, blibbelating
          and

        I wish to caret my fingers
          into their sheriff noses.

        I wish to caret my middle finger
          in their personal face-territory.

     Help me to do this
        what is necessary

to these sheriffs and clerks when I
go in to the Tippetycanoe Countatty Quarty-house
        this day.

Help me in on the marble, in the holy
oak I think, aid me in it
        in the vaultish chambers
of the quiet
rococo thing.

Help me out to call the clerks like Rambo
avoid the sodaddy swulping
of the mooching cop-cops

who WILL come slinging-O. I am Ninja.

Help me in pulling fire alarms I am Ninja.

Help me to respect God and be the handmaiden of ire Ninja.
        Help me O Helen Reddy, Ninja of the hair.

Aid me in the rococketycoco whirl
        of my fighting technique, my
disco-ball of wrath, Aid me Lord
        in the Ninja deed:

Rambo come
to me, Chuck Norris
come.
        Mad Max
I say come to me: Samson
        in Gaza, eyeless,
come—with long hair—to me

and bring thy jawbone so useful.
        Bruce Lee
where art thou, Jackie Chan
I need thy skinny justice.

Will I not fling peanuts?
             (I will fling peanuts.)
Will I not howl to scare them?
             (I will so howl.)
But what shall I say?

I will say
Who had a slapstickety mama? (Yardstick cracking whappety mama.)
Who loves the pie of his guru? (Thrown foam pie of the guru.)
What puce wing on the side of the train
belongs to the insect so pretty (Fish in clear water
hit by foam pie).

No I am not wroth with the rattlebrained Dippy doRookie
nor his sidekick either, Brenda Floribunda the excessive secretary.

Is it really my opinion
             there is something fat and abominable banging around
                          in the fata morgana
                          of our souls? Yappy

        of dogs behind me. I put the yappy of dogs behind me.

You think I would not smote him Dippy I would smote him yip.

I would smote him with my heart, buh: big flappering heartbag of coins
             right in his facety, legs smoking
                   of Dippety collapsing
                        like an cheap exchequer table it's
                        true. puh.

Remove his stapes?
Abrade his pockmarks?
Stomp on lungs?
Crack like chicken?

I am not wroth with that intestinal obstruction Dippy the Cop causing
colic vomiting and constipation no.

I am not wroth with that breach of decency Brenda the Clerk causing pulling of the skin no.

But I would smote them for a nickel.

Smack them like a spondee.

Their groans should ha-ha among the trumpets.
    puh.

HOW I CAUGHT MY COLD

And then, O God, I saw the Norsemen
rounding the bar with heavy way on.
 Between the sodden buoys, the skerries
 and cape: they came on,
  their sail down,
  they were really rowing.

And when they docked in a froth of Turkish composite arrows and faked hemp
we tried to torch the pier with pans and turf-oil,
but the dicky sun went orange in their steel-pinned strakes
 and the dock-snot fiddled tan
 in the tarred pighair of their caulking
 before I went limp
 and remembered no more.

And remembered no more until I came to,
when they told me, when they gathered round to say,
that in disembarking those boomsail tubs, the hair, their malodorous
 gear, the fur, their murderous glare
 was all too much for our battle-bred dogs,
 which, albeit small, did not fight fair.

Thus at that inglorious and rainy pier,
on our slick feet and among the abandoned sod-bombs
no one fought fair—least of all the Norsemen.
It was a classic *contra vires acrium:*
 there was nothing worser. No one remembers
 exactly in what order
 they performed the rapine and the murder—
 whether rapine then murder, or vice versa.

We only gathered that it was over,
how here and there the dogs lay punctured, be-dog-headed,
how the pigs were in the doldrums, the chickens
 looked like little pills, and that
 Piers noted foxes had come out of the hills
 to plunder our unburned larders.

But the order: we wanted to know the order:
Whether murder, rapine, rapine, murder, and *then* their tea, or porter?
Such questions we considered on the pier
                among the loose arrows and the stuck ones,
                until Eadweard the Oxherd cleared his throat
                and made it clear they had seized my book.
                They had seized my book. He made this clear.

And I tell you, John,
My eyes rolled out to where I thought Frisia was,
where the whiskery daughters of the ursi albi
                had taken my Babs,
                somewhere between the iceblink and the blasentang.
                And I longed for the shotgun

and the Armalite—cool heft
of the air-cooled rifle: sniper's Browning
with lead butt: for the dum-dum, the hollow point.
                I was tired of the town and the town's talk,
                of my butt under the harrow—
                I wanted a shotgun and a tomahawk.
                I wanted battle.

I gazed out
into the gesso and gold leaf
of all that clinks and festers in the sea—
                the cowry and geoducks, *pollos del mar,*
                the cheap and ridiculous wars
                of groupers and blowfish,

crabs who dangle
like so many teens
among the shingled cod,
                puffins and terns
                zipped up tight as freezer bags,
                gulls resting on seashine
                like so many wedding rings—

And I thought of my God
as a sunk cannon blooming with rust
among impertinent nurse sharks and tiger sharks.
             And so gazing into all of it—
             into the great sea's bric-a-brac, the daybook
             of the Northeast, and the girdle book
             of the bladderwrack—

and of the sealion heads that looked
like sealion butts—I dove in
to scan the wrackèd floor of the watermark
             for my *fides*
             and *eruditio.*
             (I, ahh: I went a little nuts.)

I swam for about a half hour and stood:
Waist-deep, penis shrunk to a bolt,
kinked bridles of seagrass wrapped broken
             on my knees in knots: I'd been following the Norsemen
             without a boat. Feeling stupid,
             though somewhat like a stud,

I strode up on the strand and stretched.
Villagers were bringing me coats.
       Well beyond my bailiwick,
       I had hunted in the waters till I came out sick:
             Remembering what I was,
             I bent down in the sand
             and made some notes.

HAIR

I balance the big convict on my head
and walk out of the prison with the inmate
beneath my bangs. My head is rather large. We
approach the guards with whom I chat amiably. They don't
suspect there is a convict on
my head. I walk through the gates to the parking
lot where I put the prisoner down and say
don't run, it might look suspicious.

The inmate and I stand in the parking lot.
He is frightened, confused
and has big hair. They are
called dreads. They are fierce and impressive
dreadlocks. He stands there before me. We shake
hands. He smiles and says to me, "You can come down now."
I say,
"What?"

And out of his dreadlocks crawl three men one
who is very fat, they all seem so happy
and nervous, I am now incredibly
nervous, I have just hidden four men in
my hair. I have aided the escape
of four large felons, now I am a medium-sized felon.
We are five felons standing in the parking
lot outside Auburn Prison, I say, "Look,
what are you doing here! we're in big
trouble, get in my car!" We drive to Ithaca.

I take them to the house of Pete Wetherbee,
a Dante professor and fellow teacher
at the prison. As he answers the door
he says, "Hi! Come in, Come in. Gosh, this is *great*
to see you! Golly, it's *very* terr-*ific* to *see* you! What day is it?" We
make small talk. Chat. We have some tea. As we
are sipping our tea, Pete uncrosses his legs and shouts: "JESUS! What the SHIT
are you doing here! You're supposed to be in prison!"

"We know," the men say in unison. "Gabe
put us in his hair. We're out now."

There is pounding at the door. Pete's wife, Judy,
runs in, says from the kitchen the house looks
surrounded. Pete blurts, "Look, get in my hair!"
"But you're balding!" we shout. "OK, get in
Judy's hair."

The inmates climb onto the head of his wife.
She staggers around, grips the sofa back. The
police enter, we say hi, Pete's wife wobbles.
The police notice, look at each other.
Pete says, "Forgive my wife, she's drunk." Judy
looks very annoyed.

She excuses herself, wobbles toward the bed-
room, says she's gotta lay down. The police
feign respect and nod in a patronizing
fashion. Their heads are so small, I think. "Look,"
says Pete, "What do you want?"

A policeman lies, "We were concerned about you
and Gabe. Four convicts escaped this afternoon."

"Jeepers," says Pete, "Well, they're not hair, I mean here."

"If you see anything, just call 911."
We nod, "Thank you, officers." They leave. We run
to the bedroom. Pete's wife meets us at the door.
She's bald. She's
enraged. Pete says,
"Where's your wig!" She slaps him, says: "There!
on the bed." On the bed is a handbag.
"It's in the handbag?" I yell. Yes in the
handbag, she says. I pick up the handbag.
I hear muffled shouts from in the handbag.
I begin weeping. I apologize to them
both. I take the handbag
home. I am still weeping. I put the handbag

in a backpack. I put the backpack in a
suitcase. I put the suitcase in a trunk.
The trunk is heavy. I put the trunk in
my hair. I walk out into the street. I hear
a wind and feeble knocking from inside
my hair. But I just keep walking. I walk,
weeping. I don't know what to do. I just
don't know what to do with the men
in my graying, auburn hair.

MY BUTTOCKS

> your buttocks
> WALLACE STEVENS

I am very interested in my buttocks,
because it is the part of my body I most infrequently see.

You might argue that if I were really interested in my buttocks
I would use mirrors and look at it more often.

But I reject that theory.
I am at once plainly interested in my buttocks,
at the same time that I look at it about once a year.

I am frankly uninterested in the buttocks of other people.
If I had but one buttocks to look at, I would prefer it be mine.
Don't construe that as evidence that I look at my buttocks but more than once a year.
Because I don't.

Indeed I would prefer it if other people didn't have buttocks.
Better two groins than one buttocks—one in front, one in back.
That way we could have our choice of groins to look at.
We could also choose to use one groin over another, either during sex
or using the bathroom. This would cut down on repair bills and maintenance costs
for our groins (urinary infections, prostate things, flaming birth canals,
yeast issues): two groins, no buttocks. Perhaps a sewer-tube that could extend down to
either foot, and at the moment of defecation we remove the shoe and give a good
            kick,
flinging the ball of excrement away from us. Bathrooms
would have to have backboards.

All of us hermaphrodites who shit from our feet. We would have banished anal sex to
our heels. Which brings me to another concern: the new anus that is now
in one of our feet: would that anus be near our toes or near the heel, or on the top of
            the foot?

My concern is this: If the anus were in the instep, would it not leave little pucker marks in our footprints?

No, I don't like buttocks. Despite rumors to the contrary. Contrary, there's a word. I oppose the word contrary.

BIRD

Come to the suet, birdy.
Come get fat.

      Come here, bulbous swift.

Come to the suet
     like a roaring hairclip.

    You have been behaving like a wacko there in the rhody,
come get fat.

I bet you wish you had a thicky bones like I.

You are nothing more than a very small ape.

You are a baby ape.

I beat you bird who flies over corn, I
beat you ape of the water.

Who can thou bite or eat or spank at now?

The day I beat up a lake geese

the wind June-cold around the heft of the chipping iron:
and 2 of the geese were making the love-paste
when I struck them dead honk.

I struck them dead honk.
The wind round the tip of my club went hoo.

I killed the ape because it thought it was the King of my potty.

It is not.

I am the King of my potty.

DEAR WOODLOUSE

Few of us have heard
your crinkling integument,

your fuss and jog
at the grease and riddled wood

that shims, as always,
the axle of the world.

Yet things drop back
into its dusty rims

through your neighborhood, routed
by your umber moods. The rain

goes up and down in your alleys

in blue, forgotten strings. Yours
is the comedy of litter, little dipshit. You

are a bursar of things. Your shadow,

a near yet winnowed guest
sewn to you with legs, shares

with all of us
the same dim signs of want and saga.

On September's humid bricks
I saw your legs upended:

the silence of a tiny orchestra
was waving bows and batons at the sun—

your shadow like a coward under you, freed,
yet clinging to your back. Maybe this

is what Augustine meant: "Cleave fast, my soul, unto Him,
for He has freed thee."

Ponderous thimble, far now
from spiders' bobbins, Crusoe

of patience: your penance
not to have one, your work

to have no faith. As for what
is in your breast: no

psychomachy or dark night, just
a thin

and labored breath—*spiritus*
nonetheless.

Sincerely,

Gabriel Gudding

THE ATHEIST GNAT

My sister runs through the door farting.
As she gallops down the hallway farting
she grows steadily lighter
until at last she is lifted upward
by the propulsion
from her anus.
She lodges against the ceiling.

Then she farts a fruit bat.
Which is in turn farting.

They bounce restless against the ceiling,
my sister and the fruit bat, each emitting
a feeble staccato.

The bat inches about
propelled as much by its anus as by its wings.

The bat farts a fly which is in turn farting.

The three farters bump around on the ceiling.
They sound like an engine tied together with a thong.

The fly mutters, I am a Mohammedan.
The bat responds, I am a Christian!
And my sister lets it be known she is a Jew.

They argue.
They grow heavy.

My sister falls to the carpet.

We look up:
in the hallway sky, the fly farts a gnat.

It is not farting.

STATEMENT

I have felt for some time that I am writing inside a butt, and that I try
very hard to articulate my exit. I feel I can never leave the butt, I
stay in it, I leave but find myself back within the butt every day. Every
day I leave and every day I find myself again within the butt. The
hopelessness of the situation is no longer infuriating to me. I used to
feel that it was a failure to find myself inside the butt time after
time. But now I look on my buttness, my in-buttness, as a kind of
testimony of durability, I feel elastic, like I can always snap right
back to the butt. Like BVDs. I am bound to it and compassed by it. I am
in the butt. And I am happy there.

I am in a butt.

REQUIEM CADENZA

for the civil libertarians who died on September 11, 2001

I shall thank John Ashcroft for being a great American,
I shall thank John Ashcroft for being a great American so well
        that there is no doubt left
        about how good great Americans are for America.

      I shall never blame America.
      Nor shall I blame America.
      Nor shall I ever think of blaming America
        or any part of America
        at any point in its history, ever.

I shall not blame the radios nor the cartoons of America, nor of Buenos Aires,
nor even of Bolivia: nor finally
        of Venezuela. Franz Liszt
shall not be blamed, nor will

Mary Baker Eddy, Eddie Haskell, Buddy Holly, Hollis Ellis, Ellen Knapp, Ella
Fitzgerald, Zelda Fitzgerald, F. Scott, Ridley Scott, Frances Scott Key, Great Scot,
Scott-Amundsen, Duns Scotus, John Donne, Don Johnson,
Dr. Johnson, Stacy Thompson,
        or Donner and Blitzen.

Nor will I single out the Baroness Blixen,
      Tom Mix, Tom Lux, Tom Thumb, Tiny Tim, Thom Gunn, Gale Gunderson,
Louise Glück, or
Elizabeth Hardwick.

Nor Maria Sedgewick or Sister Sledge. Nor the Sedulous Sisters of Mother Maria.

I shall not blame the Pope, the papists, the Pogues, the Pogue Mahones, nor the
Popes sans McGowen.

I will not blame the island of Pogo Pogo, the town of Walla Walla, Sing Sing prison,
        nor
the Hamma Hamma river.

Who then to blame if not Man Ray, Ray Kroc or Betty Crocker—the kamikaze's
"Tora! Tora! Tora!" or the matador-a's
"Toro! Toro!"

If not Okinawa, Oklahoma, or the OK Corral. If not
Lake Baikal or the Nara Canal. Or the shallow little ladle of Lake Lida near
        Sara-je-vo.

If not the op-eds of Oppenheimer
or the histories of Buttenheim,

Nor Boutras Boutras in Bío-Bío,
or Oromosto's in Oraroo (or the kangaroos either),
then who?

If not the cats in Kiti in the Kittatinny Mountains, or
Rin Tin Tin of Titicaca,
        Loma Linda,
            Osh Kosh,
                Ulladulla,
                    Van Vieng,
                        Kyzyl-Kyyva,
                            Tana Tuva
                                Ust'-Usa (that's in Russia).

If not the Thai's dog Fido in Phi Phi Kho—8 tracks, HiFi's, or indeed High 5's.
Or the Paw Paw tree either.

Or Pol Pot. Or Pol Pot's papa. Or the Yarra Yarra Lakes: Kristi Yamaguchi or
Yamaguchi, Japan.

If not
Mei-mei Berssenbrugge, John-John Kennedy, Xion Xian China, Xia-Xia
        Mozambique,
or Woy
Woy Australia (which is Way
Way down under):
If not
Bill Knott,

why not?
      If not
My Three Sons, Three Days of the Condor, Two Years Before the Mast,
Moby Dick or Mobile Gas.
If not Sonny and Cher, or Sony and Che Guevara.

If not those who play
      bingo in Durango,
            ping pong in Hong Kong,
                  baseball in Vauxhall,
                        football in Nashville, soccer
                              in Sauk Center, lacrosse
                                    in Las Cruces, tennis
                                          in Tunis, croquet in Caracas
or jai alai in Lorelei,

then why?

"Charge of the L. B.": General Bosquet made this remark while watching Lord Cardigan's unnecessary charge of the Crimean guns at the battle of Balaklava, October 25, 1854. In true imperialist fashion, Cardigan's vain and reckless act was transmuted by Tennyson into heroism.

"Dear Woodlouse": The lines "Cleave fast, my soul, unto Him, / for He has freed thee" are from Augustine's *Confessions*.

"The *OED*": Joan of Arc was actually anointed July 17th, 1429, but by the time I caught the error, the meter of this poem was set. And I would rather change history than change the meter.

"Pedagogy": Johannes Comenius is the Latin name for Jan Komensky (1592–1670), the Czech educational theorist responsible for the pernicious idea that education should be a lifelong affair. The lines "like a sage escaped / from the inanity of life's battle" are quoted from Carlyle's description of how Coleridge looked just prior to his death. The final three lines are based on Isaiah 63:1.

"Poem about My Strabismus": Strabismus—lazy eye; the condition of being cross-eyed.

"Coalman": The reference to Samson and the foxes is based on Judges 15:4.

"Fons Belli": A catalog of siege engines.

"How I Caught My Cold": Set in Lindisfarne in the ninth century.

"Hair": Pete Wetherbee's wife is actually named Andrea; and if she is anything like Pete, she is the best of people.

"My Buttocks": Epigraph taken from Wallace Stevens's "Last Looks at the Lilacs."

ACKNOWLEDGMENTS

I am grateful to William Ray Arney, Jasper Bernes, Marianne Boruch, Marina Byrne-Folan, Clio Byrne-Gudding, Leo Daugherty, Jordan Davis and the members of Subsubpoetics, Bobby Dobby, Denise Duhamel, Amy Gerstler, Roger Gilbert, Willard Greenwood, Phyllis Janowitz, Brigit Pegeen Kelly, Ken McClane, Heather McHugh, Michael Madonick, Amanda Moore, Robert Morgan, Ed Ochester, Karl Ivan Parker, Sarah Pedersen, John Poch, Rita Pougiales, Sara Rideout, Mary Ruefle, Reginald Shepherd, Stephanie Vaughn, Pete Wetherbee, Crystal Williams and, with huzzahs, Mairéad Byrne, for their advice and/or inspiration.

A. R. Ammons and Tom Andrews left this world before my first book entered it, so I hope the procurement staff of whatever library they currently frequent will see fit to request it.

Finally, I extend my gratitude to the editors of the journals and presses in which many of these poems appeared (some in earlier versions):

American Literary Review: "Daybook to Oyster, His Infant Daughter"; *American Poetry Review:* "Foundry," "How I Caught My Cold," "Infantry," "The *OED*," "The Pallbearer Races," "Pedagogy," "For Quintus Laberius Durus, Who, because of a Javelin in His Lungs, Died Near Kent, in Early August, 54 B.C.," "Requiem Cadenza," "Richard Wilbur," ["How I Caught My Cold" reprinted in *Poetry Daily*]; *Another Chicago Magazine:* "Youth of the Backhoe"; *Commonweal:* "Dear Woodlouse"; *Conduit:* "A Defense of Poetry," "Ronald Reagan"; *The East Village:* "Adolescence," "Infantry," "On the Rectum of Peacocks"; *Fence:* "Bird"; *5 AM:* "Robert Lowell," "Wish"; *Green Mountains Review:* "Adolescence," "Charge of the L. B."; *Iowa Review:* "One Petition Lofted into the Ginkgos" [reprinted in *Poetry Daily*]; *Iron Horse Literary Review:* "Bail"; *The Nation:* "The Parenthesis Inserts Itself into the Transcripts of the Committee on Un-American Activities" [reprinted in *Jacket*]; *Passages North:* "Coalman"; *River Styx:* "Bosun"; *Seneca Review:* "Tippetycanoe Delendum Est" [reprinted from *FlashPoint*]; *Sycamore Review:* "Dear Housefly."

Oasis Press published "A Defense of Poetry" and "How I Caught My Cold" in a double broadside in May 2000.

"One Petition Lofted into the Ginkgos" and "The Parenthesis Inserts Itself into the Transcripts of the Committee on Un-American Activities" appears in the anthology *A Fine Excess: Contemporary Literature at Play,* Sarabande Books, 2001.

"A Defense of Poetry" appears in *Great American Prose Poems: From Poe to the Present,* edited by David Lehman, Scribner, 2003.

GABRIEL GUDDING is an assistant professor of English at Illinois State University. He is a recipient of the "Discovery"/*The Nation* Award and an M.F.A. from Cornell University in 2000. He has initiated creative writing programs in prisons in Auburn, New York, and Holly Springs, Mississippi, and currently lives in Bloomington, Illinois.